# FLICKERS

For Morri,

with warmest thanks.
for your hospitality
and good conversation
from a friend and an
admirer of your work,

Bill

10/7/60

# FLICKERS ▪ ▪ ▪ ▪ ▪

poems by

William Trowbridge

*Wm. Trowbridge*

UNIVERSITY OF ARKANSAS PRESS

*Fayetteville*

2000

04   03   02   01   00      5   4   3   2   1

*Designed by Liz Lester*

⊛   The paper used in this publication meets the minimum requirements of the
American National Standard for Permanence of Paper for Printed Library Materials
Z39.48-1984.


LIBRARY OF CONGRESS CATALOGING-IN-PUBLICATION DATA

Trowbridge, William, 1941–
    Flickers / William Trowbridge.
        p.    cm.
    ISBN 1-55728-586-1 (alk. paper)
        I. Title.
    PS3570.R66 F55 2000
    811'.54 21—dc21              99-044257

For Robert Wallace
*1932–1999*

*poet, editor, scholar, mentor, friend*

and

William Frederick Trowbridge
*September 27, 1999*

*grandson,
on his first day in the world*

# Acknowledgements

My thanks to the following periodicals, in whose pages these poems first appeared: *Artful Dodge:* "Box Kite"; *Barrow Street:* "Gate"; *Blue Moon:* "Honey Wagon"; *The Chariton Review:* "Summer's Almost Gone," "American Primitive"; *The Chattahoochee Review:* "Shoes," "Playing Dead"; *Chelsea:* "Fall Guys," "Gotta Dance"; *Confrontation:* "In Memoriam: Duffy"; *Connecticut Review:* "Monster"; *Crazyhorse:* "At Sunset Palms"; *The Florida Review:* "Stamps of the World!"; *Flyway:* "Gorgeous George"; *The Gettysburg Review:* "The Art of Vanishing"; *The Georgia Review:* "First Book of Shadow," "Flickers," "Poets' Corner"; *Great River Review:* "His Greatest Moments," "Trip to the Middle Ages," "Curtain Call"; *The Missouri Review:* "Walking Out"; *The Nebraska Review:* "Good-by, Angel of Death"; *New Letters:* "Pale Riders," "The Fuhrer to His Eva," "Polacks," "Blood," "Smell," "Glad Wrap," "Glad to Meet You, Jesus," "Button Your Lip"; *New Orleans Review:* "Coat of Arms"; *Pivot:* "The Band Director's Farewell"; *Prairie Schooner:* "Suckers," "Uncle Miltie"; *River City:* "The Glads at Home on Memorial Day," "Glad All Over," "Glad Tidings"; *The Southern Review:* "Dog Tags"; *Spoon River Poetry Quarterly:* "Visit," "Interview" (originally titled "Dmitri"), "June Bugs," "Eating the Menu"; *Tar River Poetry:* "At the Antique Toy Museum," "Losing It"; *Yarrow:* "Hard."

My sincerest thanks also to Robert Wallace, Jonathan Holden, Jim Simmerman, David Citino, David Slater, Catie Rosemurgy, and Beth Richards, friends who lent their time and expertise to help in the making of this book. And thanks to the Anderson Center and the Ragdale Foundation, at whose accommodations many of the poems were written.

# Contents

## III ▪ ▪ ▪ ▪

## IV ▪ ▪ ▪ ▪

# The Art of Vanishing

*"I just don't put all my weight down."*
—Minnie Pearl
on airplane safety

Who's never studied it? doesn't recognize
the jittery clerk in the cartoon, who,
when the CEO rounds the corner, becomes
in rapid-fire succession a water fountain,
fax machine, filing cabinet; or the speeder who spots
the plain clothes car behind him,
and tries to slip inside absolute 55,
where, as on any such Platonic back street,
phenomenon turns noumenon and disappears?
If we get it right, it's *presto!*—not even a sleeve
for nothing to be up as we slide into
our back row desks, staring down
when the teacher's deciding who
to call on, when the specialist's scanning
for intrigue on the X-rays. When work
numbs our faces and knots our jaws, we'd
trade places with The Invisible Man, shuffling
off his clothes and bandages, free at last
to sail plates at their heads, goose the boss.
But we're more kin to that sad Coyote, concealed
with "vanishing" cream, scotched when the beer
truck driver doesn't see us, or to the proverbial
ostrich, sand in our mouths and asses up
for another proctoscope.
                "Shim-shala-bim!"
cried Harry Blackstone Jr.; "Oh," we exclaimed,

as his spangly assistant dematerialized,
transmigrated to the dusty nether world
beneath the trap door. "Dust to dust," says the preacher,
and—one, two, three—to our amazement and dismay,
an amateur, someone we actually knew,
does it lying down, without the mirrors.

# Eating the Menu

Before you try it, study the fat guy
in *Diner.* Let the word go out a week or so
before. Then unfold from your Nash Rambler
early on some Christmas shopping night
and assume your usual seat, in the booth
by the register. Wear your ordinary face,
common as puffed wheat, and hold
the chin music; just tunnel in and start
with a surprise move: the Wing Pack,
thought to be a dead end (serves six)
and a pot of caffeinated. Then advance
like winter down the county roads
of Chicken and Pork, doubling the hash browns
as chortles taper off. Angle from Beef
to Sandwiches and catch the rest of Drinks
before doubling back to unadulterated java.
Do most of this while everyone's yammering
away at one another, because the main thing's
not the hubba-hubba, and besides, let's face it,
this is not a spectator sport till toward the end.
When the chitchat's died and everybody's
gawking, cross into Desserts: the triple
fudge brownie, pecan pie à la mode,
bread pudding with Rex's own
white-raisin sauce and heavy cream.

                                             Assay
the final bite, narrowing your eyes to hint
the pudding's maybe a little stingy

on cinnamon or the sauce overstated;
then, dabbing your lips and folding up
your napkin, rise and turn away,
leaving a fat tip by your coffee cup,
ambling like Unitas did in 1958,
Colts vs. Giants, toward the lockers
as Ameche bucked that final handoff
into pay dirt, hearing the throng begin
to glorify as the snow starts up again,
feeling your image fix for generations
—for some a wallet photo to be shown
like a membership card or old school picture—
as you ease into your Rambler and turn
the key, become The Guy Who Ate the Menu.

# Uncle Miltie

"MAAAKE-UP!" yells the midget, who whaps
him in the kisser with the giant powder puff,
and, emerged from the still-expanding cloud, he shoots
his classic take at us, this time
through a mask of talc, his rouged lips
pouting, his drag smock pulled askew. It's vaudeville
schtick, ancient, laid on thick as cream pie, shoveled
high as that frowzy bouffant. He holds the pose,
sweating, waiting for the laughs to ebb. He needs
to bring the house down every night, to kill us,
knock us dead. Finally, he hits his mark, and,
batting opera lashes, lisps, "I will KEEOW you,
I will KEEOW you a MIWION times."

# Gorgeous George

*George Raymond Wagner*
*1915–1963*

He flounced into the ring like Vanity,
flicking golden hairpins at the hoots, sniffing
petulantly from a box marked "Florida Air,"
taunting the crowd toward frenzy
with his Fauntleroy strut and Harlow curls.

The meanest sissy in the game,
he specialized in the eye gouge,
the head butt, the finger stomp,
fluttering innocence when faulted,
showing fair blow with open hand
while getting in one last punt,
till time to pay the scapegoat's dues
as Verne Gagne or Lou Thesz
administered the Dutch rub
or a good, honest right cross,
and finished him with an airplane spin.

Fair play's defiler, silk purse *and* sow's ear,
he spurned the handshake, spritzed cologne,
fought the bad fight till the final fall,
when he prissed away, protesting foul,
slipping oblivion one in the kidney.

# Walking Out

*The Death of Karl Wallenda*

The wire shimmers between two buildings,
ten stories up, and a northwest wind
shoves at the balance pole he carries
like an offering. Below, a meager crowd
edges back; even the children can see
something is wrong, that the center
seems to drift from the gaunt torso
humped and swaying above those heron legs.

"To be on the wire is life, and the rest
is waiting," he said, after the Flying Pyramid
collapsed, leaving one son dead and one
with legs inert as putty. He's stayed on
sixty years, till obsolete as risk
without insurance. But today, when the wind
lifts the pole past saving, he consents
in silence to the fall, lets the wire go by
without a glance and drops easily downward,
composed upon his final shaft of light.

# At the Antique Toy Museum

To think some child once cantered back
and forth on that rag-maned hobby horse,
its one crazed eye fixed on something just
behind us, or twisted the rusty key
to make this tin train spark and click
around the tracks once more,
the painted-on passengers and crew
still settled for the long, long ride.
Such toys *were* built to last,
though most conceal some splinter,
jagged edge, protruding nail. Their story
smacks of Grimm instead of Golden Books,
of booby trap and ambush, fangs
behind this tree, that door. Among
the tiny Chippendales and sterling
in this doll house, the air is old world:
close, musty. *This* Mickey Mouse,
with his mute and rat-like countenance,
points out the minutes and the hours.

## Losing It

Ex-golden-boy, now called old at 27,
Becker's losing again, though he owned
the first two sets, probably saw
the ball arrive in slo-mo, had time
to weigh a cross court forehand against
one down the line. We watch him slump
as he double faults, nets the easy volley,
ages before us like some large begonia
shot in time-lapse. He's come down
with a disease the French call "Little Arm"
—that drawing-in to shrink the gap
between hit and mis-hit, passing
shot and unforced error. It's time
to root for someone new. When the scores
come on, we switch to Weather. No break's
in sight. A bloated low from Canada
rotates over where we live;
cold rain mats the dead leaves
down. Next up: winter. We feel it
as we turn toward bed, think of Ryan
dugout bound as the winning
run lopes across the plate.

# First Book of Shadow

Shadow keeps a water bed right inside your heart,
    with little heart-shaped pillows on it.

Shadow laughs at exactly the same jokes you do
    but doesn't really get them.

Every child has an imaginary Shadow.

Shadow thinks people who use
    umbraphobic expressions, like "shadowy"
    or "shadowing" or "lost in the shadows,"
    are just being lumocentric.
                        Can you
  say *um*-bra-*fo*-bik?

Shadow likes to hang around your playground,
    likes you just the way you are.

Sometimes Shadow likes to imagine you
    a little taller or a little shorter.

Shadow's favorite game is Tag, and you're It.
    No tags back.

Shadow's got a dog named
    Shadow. Can you find him?

Shadow and Shadow like to run fast.
    How fast can *you* run?

After a nice stay in intensive care, everybody
    gets to take home a real Shadow doll.

Someday, Shadow'll drive you over to the old neighborhood,
    where it's always cool and dark and quiet.

# Fall Guys

It's been hell all day,
and we're ready for a little
fun. And here comes Fields,
up for a big breakfast
of Haig & Haig, about
to meet the roller skate
Baby Leroy left
on the dining room floor.
Better yet, here's Keaton,
shoving off in that newbuilt
do-it-yourself yacht
he thinks is going to take him
somewhere. Or how about Stan
and Ollie trying to get a grip
on the concert grand
they've got to lug
clear up that bluff.
This is gonna be good.
Real good. We rubberneck it
from our chairs, like when we
slowpoke by a car wreck—
only this time we get
to see the crash, too,
thanks to the easy math
involved: fool + breathing
= pain and/or shame. We've
learned it by heart, remember

that little twinge before
our foot slipped, before our boat
turned belly up. But now
the laugh's on those guys,
like a bad case of hives, and just
tell us this: if they're so
rich, why ain't they smart?

## His Greatest Moments

In the 60-second spot, he's back
to dance and Rope-a-Dope and sting,
turning couplets fast as Cyrano—Clay
proclaimed Ali, flashy in Everlasts,
loose and pretty, his own brass band,
who could be watching with us now,
guard dropped as the blows rain in.

# June Bugs

At night
they thumb

against the screen door,
buzzing their wings,

fumbling about,
too dumb or hungry

to learn the problem,
bumping, probing

till they see stars
and curlicues

and drop
onto the steps,

their legs scribbling
to beat the count.


Suckers
for the left jab

with a rolled-up
magazine, they

come back
every night

till fall,
guard too low,

bottom
of the ticket,

who'll never
have the moves,

who stick out
glass jaws

and heave
their butts

around the ring
—big sad pugs

with the hearts
of famous lovers.

# Gotta Dance

We had to laugh: the bricklayer passing by
his hod as he hitch-kicks up the alley,
the teamster curbing his rig to shuffle
off to Buffalo; the hack, gob, and lugger
leaping *tour jeté* in tandem, hitting
the splits together square in the middle
of Tenth and State—ludicrous till Kelly
made us see, as Brueghel did,
that those of us who lift and haul, pry
and join, measure and cut, who sweat
for wages, who wear loose pants and heavy
shoes, are dancers too, can pirouette
in rainy gutters, arabesque among
the trash cans, waltz with night sticks, rumba
over washtubs, buck and wing our way
right up the loading ramp and kneel
with arms outstretched in a Broadway finish,
hearts replete on our flannel sleeves.

# Summer's Almost Gone

The squirrels are spreading the rumor: no more monkey business.
The Dow Jones hops up, then down, then back up, trying for attention,
    up against dog days.
The Capitol dome rattles like a witch doctor's gourd. "More Republicans,"
    warn the talking drums.
The networks labor underground to stockpile T, A, and blood capsules
    for Sweeps Week, when all hell won't be enough to save some.
Pedestrians slip into light coats of pollen and mold spores.
The *Enquirer* reports the sighting of Satan's image over Chicago during
    the heat emergency. His words were, "For the hottest deals in town,
    see Sal at Mutto's Chevrolet on East Wacker."
The old elms shrug: "You think this is hot? We could tell you about hot."
Wal-Mart and Kmart burgeon into crooked towers of back-to-school candy.
    They're heaven-bound, via the moon. Greeters offer themselves
    to the lowest common denominator. There's a Blue-Light on moon caps.
Representatives from Tire City have announced they intend a hostile
    takeover and cleansing of their former territory, now known
    as Carpet City. Furniture City will not intervene.
The NFL's negotiating for rights to the Baptist Church.
The carnies have packed up the Tilt-a-Whirl and Ferris wheel, leaving us
    up to our ass in free parking.
Everyone under 30 dreams of shoplifting some Air Jordans for school.
Everyone over 30 dreams of going to prison for shoplifting.
The hypochondriacs wake up noticing little dark spots in front of their eyes,
    think they could be in the middle of something serious.
"Winterize now," say the prime time commercials. "Spend, spend, spend!"
    cry the cicadas and katydids over the scorched, moonlit lawns.

# Flickers

"Johnny, what I done wrong?"—last words
of Pancho Villa, spoken to a gringo pal
after one of a thousand would-be avengers
shot straight; or, rather, Wallace Beery's words
to Stuart Erwin at the end of *Viva Villa,*
or the guy's who wrote the screenplay, though
they probably weren't *his* last words,
or the real Villa's. But who could have said it
better, whoever said it? Not Bogie,
lying nearly mummified by cancer,
not Marilyn, awash in Seconal,
not Fonda, dying as he played a guy
who's dying, or the now-dead Wallace Beery,
Stuart Erwin, and that screenwriter. We can't
keep track: our favorite movies fill up
with the walking, talking dead, the ghosts
of ghosts, Platonic shadows thrice removed
from sunlight. They knew us back when we
were sharper, showed us how to walk
and smoke and kiss, how acting
can make things seem more real than real
could ever seem. Now we're strangers,
trying to act like nothing's really changed,
and the Wicked Witch—the one that Judy,
playing Dorothy, pretended to dream up
in the movie—who was really nice
old Margaret Hamilton and didn't really die
till 1985, is really, *really* dead.
Bogie, Pancho, Johnny, what we done wrong?

## American Primitive

Here comes Ollie on a dead run,
his tonnage bounding half a step behind.
Stan's eyes bat an SOS as he tries to decide
if he should run, too. Too late! It's Anger,
dense as a beer truck, about to take the corner
where even *he'd* notice Stan's just accidentally
knocked the radiator off his new Lizzie, the one
Anger was about to gas up and take Sex out
for some sex in. Meanwhile, Sex, finished
dolling up in her feathery boudoir, sashays
out the very same door Stan's in front of.

You got it: WHAP, she legs it into his arms
as he stands there blubbering about the radiator
and Anger runs across the whole admittedly
suspicious scene. Now here comes Ollie,
back to see what's kept Stan, but,
LOOK OUT! he slams right into Sex.
Anger's little fuse whispers faster, his eyes
zeroing in above the wingspan of his moustache.

Stan and Ollie have a tough time explaining
how all this happened innocently. They reveal
their dreams, beatific, harmless as miniature
sailing ships in bottles. Anger, beside himself,
declares Sex off limits and hurls the dreams
to the curb. Ker-SMASH, go Ollie's; tinkle, goes Stan's.

Now Sex's mother, Domesticity, a hillock
of cheeks and love handles, barges out
choked up on a rolling pin long enough
for the Babe. What's all the ruckus about,
she demands, not about to believe a syllable.

Look, mimes Stan, our dreams are smashed again,
and *he* (Stan steals a brave glance at Anger) did it.
Brutes! huffs Domesticity, taking check swings
at our boys, who duck and dive till Authority

marches up stiff-backed as a brigadier
and, letting Sex and Anger waltz off arm in arm,
charges the shy duo with creating a disturbance
by being a couple of powerless chumps. Alerted,
Contempt itches to gavel down their plea.

It's *another* fine mess Stan's gotten them into,
to quote Ollie, though after hopping a bus for Lompoc
when Authority gets distracted by Sex and Anger
blasting through the stoplight right under his nose,
they sleep like baby millionaires, while, far away,
halfheartedly, Death bullies his kettledrum.

II

# Glad Wrap

After the Cowboys lick the Lions on TV,
the Glad family, young and old, hunkers down
at close quarters in their love warehouse
for Thanksgiving dinner, never talking
with their mouths. They stunt like linebackers
around the big, dead, buttery tom, Mamaw
probing for a clear shot at the white meat. Dad
used to throw an insurmountable crack-back,
cutting through Sis like choo-choo beans,
till Mrs. I. M. Glad, his wife since
that terrible accident, got certified
by a real psychiatrist, and little Titus Glad,
who's turned into an incurable taxidermist
and might just as well wear high heels
for all he knows about the bump and run,
figured out which end was actually up. Now
they can punch Dad a ticket to Queer Street
and have enough left to hit the nearest
eatery, wade through a shitload of buffalo
wings with not so much as a granule
of meat tenderizer, and waltz out smelling
like twin bars of soap on a rope. You shake
or you bake, is the way they put it, French
dip or total immersion. We call that "family,"
and there's nothing makes a holiday meal
much tastier, even when you can't get
your shorts back on with a power winch
hooked to twenty feet of new hemp.

# The Glads at Home on Memorial Day

Ho hum: Grandpa's head's come off
again and Sis, who was using it
as a conversation piece, won't put it back on
straight, even for a couple of hours
of quality time. "Goo!" she retorts.
"Para*keet!*" The old boy's steamed, his aorta's
thin as a herniated condom. Since when
did she learn to style hair and talk like
some Brazilian hussy. Stuck-up bitch. Finally,
Dad hears the commotion, and wheels in
that Monkey Ward gun he ordered
out of the spring catalog to protect
against joy riders. But of course,
legally blind, he aims right
of center, blowing off Sis' good leg
and parting Grandpa's fancy do right up
the back so he walks shell-shocked
as the bride of Frankenstein: ka-donk,
ka-donk, ka-donk. But don't kid
yourself: there's a lot of love here. When the smoke
clears, it's back to Tab A and Insert C,
with the instructions so Nipponized
you can't tell right from reft with a pair
of triple bifocals. And those little bitty
submarines. Like toys. No wonder
we lost the goddamned War.

# Glad to Meet You, Jesus

Grandpa Glad says his lucky
Joy Buzzer, which he ordered out of
the Johnson and Smith catalog on July 12,
1953, and which he's ever since stored
around his neck beside Saint Christopher,
tells him to obey Satan at all times,
or that maybe Satan speaks personally
*through* the Buzzer, which makes it
possessed instead of actually Satanic,
or that the whole thing's inside *him,* so
Grandpa's either possessed or Satan. "How
do you do, Mademoiselle?" he lisps, bowing
to Mamaw, giving her hand a good buzz
till she decks him with that big purse
she lugs around for civil defense. The kids
can't get enough of it. It can make them titter
all through church. They'll never forget
the time it went on in the car all the way
to Yellowstone. Dad won't either. He'd like
to see them all burn up. Grandpa says
it's Satan makes him think that, but Mamaw
says it's just good common sense. "Well then,
how do you do, Mademoiselle," says Satan.

# Glad All Over

Marsupial Glad, Titus' former brother, had a chemistry set
Dad Glad made for him out of leftover toxic material
from the garage and explosives he borrowed from where
they were putting up the new bypass. Anyway, one night
he decided to impress his mother, Mrs. I. M. Glad, who does not
usually take the slightest interest in the stage and screen, by playing
Dr. Jekyll and Mr. Hyde, mixing a cupful of nitro with a quart
of Everclear to create the "potion." Damn near got it all down, too,
except that Sis, who is known to be the jealous type as well as
the different drummer type, touched him off with her Zippo,
precipitating a detonation followed by a solemn burial
in a black and gold thermos bottle. Sis' stutter stopped
almost completely, though some say she'd been faking it.

# Gladiola

A sore subject around the Glad household
is Felonia, Marsupial's twin sister and the Glad
black sheep, who Mrs. I. M. Glad believed
till too late that she had named after some sort
of intelligent-looking floral spray she remembered
seeing on Judge Wapner. Hardly the flower, Felonia
turned out more like a wolverine, what with
those spandex toreadors and running roughshod
over her Christian upbringing and the neighbor lad,
who then began talking like a half-wit and, only after
years of rehabilitation, became a Shriner. Felonia
as good as said she cared not one whit, that she
considered herself a regular Charles Manson
of the fairer sex, whose maidenhood would go to naught
but the low-life murdering kind, and social skills
go hang. "A rose by any other name,"
quotes Mamaw, clucking her tongue.

# To Be or Not to Be Glad

Mrs. I. M. Glad allows she did not always feel dry
under the big Glad umbrella, that sometimes she dreamed
of standing by and watching the whole family, right down
to her favorite-though-fatally-detonated son Marsupial,
rotisseried by disturbed foreign torturers, who place
absolutely no value on human life—except, of course,
for torturing purposes, or for purposes of
helping with torture, which usually requires
teamwork, or for making torturer babies who will
grow up to keep torturing a lifetime employment
option—all of which is basically to admit that
*realistic* torturers *have* to place some kind of value
on human life. She had the mob-style execution
of Dad Glad himself in the pipeline, so to speak,
but, on account of being discriminated against
as a liberal, she could not pass the credit check and so
had to be satisfied with paying cash for a few
anonymous phone threats, which he pooh-poohed. Of some
consolation has been her Chihuahua, Viral, though she
had to have the little thing poisoned and stuffed due to
a flare-up of her nervous allergies. Lately, even with her folks,
Mamaw and Grandpa, around to clean up, she thinks
she'd like to live somewhere less advanced,
or maybe get her veins stripped and go into clothes.

# Glad Rags

You haven't really seen a sight till you've seen
the Glads all dolled up, ready for a grand opening,
a last look at the deceased, or just an old-time
family chowdown. Dad puts on those funny
glasses with the big pink nose and the bushy
black moustache, leaving everything else
up to your imagination. "Nyuck, nyuck,
nyuck," he quips, doing Groucho completely
wrong, while Mrs. I. M. Glad makes a face
like Madame Tussaud on half-price night,
sneezing in miniature and flicking at her nose
with that lace hanky. Grandpa and Mamaw
usually try to pass as Bobby and Cissy
from the Lawrence Welk reruns, which always
gets Little Titus' goat. His ensuing ugliness
is loud enough to wake his ex-brother Marsupial,
or what's left of him, right out of a perfectly
good thermos. Sis tries to compensate for her
tendency to hyperventilate due to low self-esteem
by getting out her tasseled boots and twirler batons,
overcorrecting with a skirt short enough for you
to see clear to East Islip. Her rendition of moonrise
has been known to bring out the men in blue,
as if she wasn't perfectly aware of that fact.

# Dad Glad Has a Conniption

Must have been the skunky Bud or Fluffy
pissing down a furnace vent again or Felonia
totaling another rental Cherokee. Anyway,
he's about to come out of his TV lounger,
the one with deep heat and Magic Fingers,
hollering at Dan Marino to take the dress off,
to get the long bomb up and try to force it
into sudden death, for Christ's sake,
if he's got the balls. "Might as well be listening
to a yellow Chinaman," Mamaw grumbles, knitting
Grandpa's shirtsleeve to the couch. "KONG POW,"
Dad retorts, stretching his eyes back with his fingers.
"MOUSY TONGUE." Mrs. I. M. Glad counters
with his least favorite ballad, "Muskrat Love,"
belted sassy as the Mormon Tabernacle Choir
could do in their Tabernacle. It's kid gloves
off now, so when Mamaw pulls her left hook
and brings a bolo clear from the Dry Tortugas,
Dad unwraps the boat horn he's been hiding
for a rainy day. Three shorts and a long,
and that, as they say in polite society, is that,
though it could just as well be Brahms to Grandpa.

# Glad Tidings

It's Christmas once more, and Dad Glad thinks
he's Bob Cratchit in the scene right after Scrooge
gives him the big goose, though he's probably got
Cratchit mixed up with somebody else,
the way he runs around grabbing women's
behinds like he was some kind of guy
from the state. The family hasn't seen him
for days; they've even discussed slipping off
to Perth Amboy to maybe knock over
a branch bank or a Dunkin' Donuts. "Let's see
some tit!" he barks, right before catching something
else where it really hurts. If this was happening
in a stupid movie the family was watching, they'd
start doing their chimp laughs. Meanwhile the woman
he'd hoped to scare into a free feel strolls off
la-de-da. "Same to you," he mumbles,
about as discouraged as stinkweed in full bloom.

# Monster

"Frrriend," pronounces Karloff amid the scent
and burble of lamb stew, leaning forward
in the wooden chair, shaping his mouth
to match the old man's. The growl subsides

and the stitched-on felon's hands unclench
as he turns the word over like a shiny stone
he's just discovered in a river bed, turns us
back toward whatever first blind hand

drew us from the forest to the little hearth
and softened our heart with fiddle and cigar. The music
warmed us and the smoke teased our throat till we
made a grin, stomped our boot, puffed

like the train from Nuremberg. "Friend GOOOD!"
we growled, shaking the floor, reaching for the fire.

# Shoes

*at the United States Holocaust Memorial Museum*

No longer stacked to warehouse ceilings,
now spread on both sides of a walkway
through a narrow hall, at first they look
like reproductions, like those castings
from the Majdenek Table or the oven doors
at Belsen. No size too small,
of course; and the high-heels, some with fabric,
were they mostly carried? Now and then
an odd pair, side-buttoned or club-soled. Though each
recalls the contours of its occupant—the thumb-sized
bunion, the septic toe—they fit together
snug as a jigsaw puzzle, but without
the picture prize—only a relief of dusky
convolutions, a magma landscape.

## The Fuhrer to His Eva

There are these spells sometimes, where I forget
you even breathe when you have to be away
from me, that you're not hanging somewhere
in a bedroom closet, with my uniforms and gloves,
pressed and waiting for the next time I,
like the hand inside a puppet, animate you.

Where else should you be? Frankly, I'm
a little shocked by signs of tampering
—new earrings, the odd smudge—when I take you
off the hanger. Time to change the locks?

And why that nonchalance when I feel
my voice stopped with our martyred soil? How
will you, all the blathering volk, exist
when I'm in hell? You'll simply vanish, all,
like those Jews I don't hear falling in the forest.

# Honey Wagon: An Historical Poem

As the Battle of the Bulge subsides, the real one,
not the wide-screen operetta, a squad of new guys
files along a frozen road to Bastogne, the bloodstain's
center. That's my father, thirty years my junior,
with the captain's bars. I'd guess their feet feel numb,
that they've never been this cold this long. Do they think
of lovers? family? steak? their Ford convertible? of Jesus
bleeding on the cross? of where they'd want their million
-dollar wound (left arm? left lung?)? Three months
of chicken shit, and today they step into the ancient
course of humans turning one another
into sudden waste.
                         Speaking of which, here comes
some, bumping along on what the Belgians call
a "honey wagon," made to haul manure. But today
it's frozen battle dead in a chin-high jumble
of dumb gesticulations. The so-named wagon's
double coat of irony is probably lost on those
still walking, who, unlike us, aren't safe
or warm enough to notice even symbols
blatant as the one lumbering down this road.

My father, too old to draft but called up anyway,
will live to eighty, which means he's bulletproof
for now. I'd like to tell him. He can't believe
how fast they shipped him here from the bubble
of Columbia, Missouri,
                              where I, four, my sister,
fifteen, and my mother, thirty-six, are listening

to Jack Benny being robbed. "Your money
or your life, I said," repeats the gunman
for the third time. "I'm thinking," says Jack,
to recorded laughter.
                  Meanwhile, maybe
my father notices the sorry load's shifting
closer to the edge with every bump, wonders
if he shouldn't stop to tell the driver before
the whole mess slides onto the road. But
what's the use, really, and he has to keep
in file and wants to stay a moving target.

So the corpses and their pale replacements pass
each other, though some will meet again tomorrow,
and, after Benny says good night, the announcer
on my family's Philco tells civilians,
including the four-year-old who'll one day
write this poem we're in, to do their share
by saving cans and buying bonds. And History,
its latest load delivered, kills the light.

# Good-By, Angel of Death

*on the final verification of the death of Nazi doctor*
*Joseph Mengele, nicknamed "The Angel of Death"—*
*accomplished in 1992 by matching DNA samples*
*from the blood of his son Rolfe with those from*
*remains found buried outside São Paulo*

Ding, dong, the wicked bastard's dead,
most assuredly, overwhelmingly,
verified-by-DNA-test dead. Throw out
that grainy snapshot of the figure
lurking along some street in Paraguay, Brazil,
or Argentina; for some, in all three
simultaneously. Forget the tabloids'
bold-face whispers of a hatchery for Hitler clones
in São Paulo or freezers packed with Aryan
louts suspended for their Fuhrer's second coming,
schemes, they say, concocted in the brain pan
of that skull we see matched in the forensic photo
half and half with the tautly grinning flesh
from 1944. How confidently he stares
from either side, the eyeball and the empty socket,
assessing us as if we'd just stepped
onto the ramp at Birkenau.
　　　What's crouching out there
in the forest, little ones? Not witches or winged
monkeys, but something storytellers never
dreamed of. The sounds are muffled and what's burning
doesn't smell like wood. But never mind:
those helixes extracted from the living blood
are carbon copies of what they say uncoiled
from deep within the worm-tracked skull and bones.

# Interview

*"The Terror, in other words, was part of a social experiment . . . with the ultimate goal of producing a nation of human robots programmed to love only the state."*

—Ian MacDonald, *The New Shostakovich*

He stares from the thicket of his cunning
through horn-rimmed saucer lenses, small
steppes owl, alert for the chance to dart
for deeper cover. Ensconced on the dark
oak chair of his supremacy, Mountain
Eagle, Wise Father, People's Leader
of Genius, Friend of Children, Reformer
of the World bows to light his avuncular
pipe, the suction sounding like vast applause
or a rifle volley deep in the forest. His words
are simple, soft, framed to be agreed with,
the Mona Lisa smile indifferent as a leveled
pistol with one round in the cylinder.

In every province, bodies jerk and flop
into their self-dug graves. The sweetish smoke
uncoils across the dossier. Behind those lenses,
the scherzo for the Fifth unfolds, its menace
theme blaring, the brass in goose step
with the lower strings as death's
broad knuckles drum the heavy desk.

## Pale Riders

The kick's that "Who the . . . !" look in the final reel,
where Bad, eyebrows raised and shoulders drooped,
figures out just who he picked to pick on this time:
not that meek-kneed practice dummy Good,
with his hymnal and his pardon-me's,
but Mr. Eye-for-Eye himself, the pale-horsed
look-alike with bony stare for whom
another town has grown too small. Some
thinning-out, his specialty, is called for,
some Bible justice, writ on our behalf
on Bad, his chattel, his children
and his children's children's children,
with Winchester and Navy Colt,
with mushroom cloud and smart bomb.

# The Packing House Cantata

*Cudahy Packing Co., Omaha, 1958*

## 1. Hard

A high school kid working
Hog Cut at the packing house
for summer cash, I'd pass them,
lined up near the front gate,
solitary, hands in pockets,
hunched in the morning heat
against the chill of drastic
lucklessness, looking otherworldly
as those German prisoners
the Russians filmed in snowy
black and white, their eyes
averted, their gray faces
slack in surrender.
Not just out of work
but made to wait for it
in public every morning till
a foreman stepped out
and announced, "I'll take you and
you and you. No more today,"
and closed the door—this
in days so flush that overtime
was often mandatory. "Fuck it,"
we'd agree when word came down
we'd have to stay till 9
again—four more stinking hours

and dinner in that cheesy cafeteria.
How we must have looked to them,
if they looked at us at all.
Once I saw one shuffle over
to the gate and take a piss
right where the morning shift
was driving in, though mostly
they'd stand or lean, occasionally
sprawl. Dismissed, they'd
have to kill another day,
dully stewing at the track
or Jerry's Reno Tap, or maybe
home spoiling the old lady's
afternoon. Here, where almost
any type or function,
esteemed to past revolting,
had a name—sticker, lugger,
stoolie, D.P.—and even
broken bones were funny, there was
no name for these, no patter.


## 2. Gate

Across the street
from the ledgers and lapels,
it opened at six-thirty,
closed after second shift,
tall as a floodgate,
ponderous as a foreman's soul,
its close, gray bars
the daily welcome

to the vast machine
of labor. You walked in.
You walked out. In time,
as with the smell and noise
and pools of guts,
you didn't notice.
One morning I saw
a newborn lamb,
brought down
from the kill floor
into the light.
It wobbled there, pinkish
and drooling, its eye in shock,
while the trucks rumbled in,
swirling the dust.
It was gone by break time.


## 3. Knife

Stubby, long, straight, curved,
hooked, it said, "Skilled."
"Good wage." "No need
for brawn." Whetted
and honed till it could
glide through rib or shank,
it sometimes turned against
the inattentive. Stickers
had a little hooked one they'd
flick in and pull through
the carotid. When a thrashing
hog kicked Peewee's

out of his hand, it sliced
across his arm so deep
the bone showed. Use it right
and it could get you more
than just respect: Leroy
up in Hog Cut got to where
he'd whip that double-handled,
semicircle blade across
a fatty loin and there'd be
nothing but the purplish sheen
of meat in membrane. Nobody
took his chair at lunch
or later, at the Mohawk.

## 4. Smell

It could carry 15 miles
in a steady wind. Inside
the gate, it gathered
almost dense enough to see,
this hodgepodge brewed
from spills of every mammal
fluid, piss-thin to tallow-
thick, multiplied
by every stage of slipping
back to dust, from fresh
up on the kill floor
to day-old chilled,
where carcasses were cut
and dressed, to festering

in drains to sifting off
of boot soles. Add to those
the peculiar stews concocted
in the hog scald, smoke room,
and down that hole
where they dropped
the slithery hides. I'd get
used to one, and another
three would crowd
against me on the way
to take my break. "That's how
*you'd* smell," a moonlighting
evangelist in Beef Kill
told me once, rinsing
his hand, offering
his other Twinkie.


## 5.  Bad

"What lets a 80-pound dog
run off a 200-pound man?"
Vernie asked me my first week
on the job. "Pull a knife, show
your .357, your karate card,
warn he could get the chair:
dog don't give a shit," he said,
nodding faintly toward a bald guy,
sleepy-eyed, baby-cheeked,
smoking alone beside
the pop machine. "Nobody

fucks with him," said Vernie,
like we were seeing Jesus
or the trip wire on a Claymore.
"Not even Ed. That's Hubert:
he don't give a shit."


## 6. Fuck

No longer word, more
like the smell, so thick
and constant the natives
didn't notice; more like
a language: "Fuck." "Fuck you."
"You fuck." "Fuck you, you
fuck." "Fuck *you*, fuckhead,
you fucking fuck fucker."
It could rise to sound amazement,
satisfaction, even love,
but it liked the bottom, growing
whiskered, deformed,
and vaguely fecal, meaning
what D.P. Richard did
to his uncle's horse, what
Bubble Ass down in Sausage
tried on blow-up dolls, what,
in the breathiest falsetto,
they all insisted my "little
girlie" and I did "Bowser style"
in the back seat of my father's
Buick, or what the ones

too putrid, crazed,
or stupid to get women
meant when they talked
about going "Oscar Wilie"
Saturdays in the alley behind
the L Street Tap. The language
was Fuck, which you had to
speak without an accent.


## 7. Blood

Not what I saw in *The Brides of Dracula*
or on my Kleenex or symbolized
in teeny glasses at the church,
it spilled, ran, dripped, crusted up
on overalls and boots,
made a four-inch pudding
on the Beef Kill floor, which took
all night to clean. The hogs
were worst: their astounded hearts
pumped two-foot gushers
as they hung in fours, flailing
on the shackle rail, sounding
almost human. The sheep
let it saturate their wool
without a sound, with only
the slightest flinch. They seemed
to offer their necks. It went
in fertilizer, dog food,
sausage. Walleye Paul would

cup his hand and drink some
for his heart. But most got pumped
into the river, which stank
all summer but never turned red.


## 8.  Polacks

Below Negroes,
my parents told me,
D.P.s up from Europe's
sewers, born to wrestle
broom and bucket, hod
and pry bar, the Slavic
tongue coarse as privy talk.
Their neighborhoods sprawled
around the packing houses,
babies yowling at St. Stephen's,
geezers and crones gobbling
oatmeal at the Polish Home.
And those weddings: Jesus,
the racket! Caravans
of heaps honked and rutted
up our street as if they owned it,
trailing streamers, shoes,
flaccid grins, careening
toward the knackwurst and Pilsner,
the whoop of that primal Catholic
urge to populate, passing us by
with their luscious secret.

## Trip to the Middle Ages

Think of it like this: the other tourists gone,
your MasterCard picked up, the last six
centuries still a twinkle in the All-Seeing.
Instead, fleas, grime, hunger, sores,
rot. And all that stuff on "Creature Feature"
real to you as shadows stretching from the forest.
It gets cold, it gets hot, it stinks
like shit, like feet, like last week's mutton.

But tonight the king, that lousy bastard,
has called for light and music, your drum to stir
the doldrums from his heart. The hall's
gone bright with lute and horn, the buzzing
of the sweaty guests, the juggler's aplomb.
Beat on, wise churl, as if these guttering candles
feed on mirth. Look! The acrobats!

# Supply and Demand

*"Jaw Breaker—2 for Each Cents"*

Skrija's Groceries, Omaha, 1949

Vaulted and shadowy as the forests in our Grimm books
or the bomb-dismantled Europe we glimpsed in *Life,* it whispered
scarcity and blackout, with its dark-stained wood and incandescent
lights, its one-brand choices, its ceiling-high shelves, hand deep,
with pole-mounted gripper for items out of reach, its silences.

They descended daily from rooms upstairs, Mr. and Mrs.,
rucked and swarthy, slight as the scents of coffee and bakery,
fruit and must, tending us well, who'd stop there after school
to browse the candies heaped in a row of glass-fronted bins
long enough to hold Snow White, our nickels ready,
our fingers tingling for jaw breakers, gum balls,
licorice, and chocolate drops, for carney-colored syrup
in tiny wax bottles, for those hemispheric nips attached
to strips of paper. We were Hansels and Gretels, with the witch
burned up in Germany, our mothers clipping recipes
in our savory homes, the Skrijas portioning our sweets,
like diamonds and rubies, into little white sacks, charmed
for us with mahogany and thrift in their dark corner store

till the supermarket came, conjured on the vacant lot
where the dairy used to be. Waxy and fluorescent,
its aisles ran on for what seemed blocks: rack on rack
of candy bars, pyramids of cookies, seven brands
of chocolate cake, a 12-foot freezer just for ice cream. It was
our right, our fathers' war gold, our air-conditioned future,

bright and germ-free as the Ice Capades. We helped
ourselves, touched and took, licked and gobbled and grabbed
for more—nougat, fudge, caramel, peanut; cherry, grape,
strawberry, lime; fructose, glucose, diglicerides—forgetting
our mothers, whose faces turned to clay, forgetting the Skrijas,
sent back to Dobrovnik, their small store emptied out,
then changed one night to a yellow bunker with barred windows,
rivet-studded door, and a sign announcing "Guns 'n' Ammo."

We've grown old and have to squeeze into our britches. But we can't eat
enough to stop this late-night gnawing as the talk shows chuckle
and we nod above our snacks, hearing scratches at the bedroom door,
or whispers, maybe, mournful and in some foreign tongue.

■ ■ ■ ■ ■ IV ■ ■ ■ ■

# Playing Dead

*(on being told my boyhood best friend was dying)*

For a moment I mistook it for a recess
back to Hickory Street, where daily we
transmogrified from cowboys to gangsters
to jaguar-eyed Marines as we rehearsed
the deaths of stars—the Duke's straightforward
flop, Bogey's slo-mo expiration,
Cagney's fuck-you snarl—choreographed
with bayonets and pistols my father
packed home from the War. No one wanted
to survive, to stand there with the humdrum
living, upstaged as the moribund gloried
in their pirouettes and sprawls, their gasps
and bucklings. Such contrast with the quick,
indifferent resurrections, with our doses
of Scripture and arithmetic. We took turns,
since someone had to live.

                      It was just
his turn to die, mine to stop and study.

# Stamps of the World!

A kid could buy them through the mail
from the Keystone Co., Crown Point, Ind.,
for six quarters and a dime: assortments
of 300, pungent as old books, exotic
as prestidigitation. I sorted, I counted,
I searched and cataloged, bought and traded,
hinged and mounted in sets and singles,
blocks and sheets: Norge, Belgique,
Fiji, Magyar; Venus, Toucan, Buddha,
Goebbels; rectangle, triangle, square;
red and blue, chartreuse and heliotrope;
Olympiad, Labor Day, Sesquicentennial,
and always the rumor of the rare find,
the one the sorters back in Crown Point
missed—that U.S. Air Mail with the biplane
printed upside down. Or could it be
the one I found, like new but with
a portrait of the Czar—a sure thing,
maybe: the secret door, the magic
beans, that crisp, uncanceled rush
I still recall when I hear the mailman
clunk the lid or watch the sun descend
bright as a block of Congo diamonds.

# Dog Tags

My closest playmates got to try them on,
my father's amulet, plain as Ike, taciturn
as Stalin, egalitarian as a Zippo: name
and serial number, stamped in steel
and hung around the neck. The notched end
fits between the two front teeth when the tag's
inserted lengthwise in the corpse's opened
jaws. Then, cold wafer made for gnawing
by the not-so-quick, it's driven deep
into the upper gum by a blow beneath
the chin. Once, alone and lost inside
his helmet in our furnace room, I closed
my eyes and opened wide, clamped it
lightly in my teeth, tasting its bitter coat
of oxidation, the salty grit embedded in the letters
and the numbers, the chill of its perfect fit.

# Button Your Lip

I learned to do it early,
through home study,

before I could
tie my shoes,

before it got
buttoned for me,

because I knew
what was good

for me, because
I was a little pitcher

with big ears,
a little Sad Sack,

who needed to
*verstehn sie*

*mach schnell.* Silence
was golden, a holy

shield that saved
my father's ship

from those loose lips,
a shelter from his rages,

a short blade
for use in close.

## Poets' Corner

They put me in right field
because I didn't pitch that well
or throw or catch or hit,
because I tried to steer the ball
like a paper plane, watched
Christmas gifts with big
red ribbons floating through
the strike zone, and swung
at dirt balls. So they played the odds,
sent me out there in the tall grass
by the Skoal sign, where I wandered
distant as the nosebleed seats
my father got us in Comiskey Park,
my teammates looking
remote and miniature,
their small cries and gesticulations
like things remembered
from a dream. I went dreamy,
sun on my face, the scent
of sod and blue grass, the lilt
of bird call and early cricket
bending afternoon away
from fastballs and hook slides
to June's lazy looping
single: baseball at its best,
my only fear the deep fly
with my name on it,
meteoric as Jehovah

or coach Bob Zambisi
closing in to deliver once
again the meaning of the game:
what it takes to play, why I had to
crouch vigilant as a soldier
in combat, which he never
had the privilege of being,
and stop that lolling around
with my head up my ass,
watching the birdies and picking
dandelions like some kind of
little priss, some kind
of Percy Bitch Shelby.

# Alien

At school they called that big one on your nose
or forehead a "third eye." Mine would pass
from glare to glower every time they announced
a dance or party; the Clearasil would fissure
like a dry creek bed. At the bathroom mirror, I'd try
to stare it down, always blinking first. Squeeze it
and you'd get acne, Mother warned. I'd seen
Buzz Lukins, transferred to our high school
for using pliers on a classmate's thumbs. His face
was stretched across the purple welts, which looked
malignant as the poxes in the sci-fi flicks where the boy
who brushes against the goo from Planet X
becomes the Creature with a Thousand Eyes. I watched
mine turn to little craters when the cores slipped out:
Moon Man, they'd call me, Pineapple, some name
like they gave to Dorothy Koncle, who bore that livid
birthmark splashed across her face, who spoke
only when spoken to, if then. I'd said it once:
"Polkadottie," after she'd walked past in the hall,
my friends and I exchanging smirks. Now I wept
for me, displaced, I thought, from sock hops, lavalieres,
and tartan cummerbunds, wrongfully marooned
with her and Buzz on the planet Other, which really
did exist, my Earth adrift like a little blue balloon.

# Coat of Arms

My father bought it through the mail.
It was made in York,
Nebraska, by old-world-type craftsmen.
It was the real thing.
It was the ideal thing.
It was turning things around.
It was suitable for framing.

It had a motto: *Sit Pons Firmus.*
It had a bridge with arches in fess gules,
    streams transfluent purpure,
    and a tower with thereon a fane argent.
It had an accompanying pamphlet authenticating everything
    and saying that Thomas Trowbridge came here in 1620
    and that the motto means "The Bridge Sits Firmly."
It had an order form for a deluxe frame or a plain one.
It had all the right equipment in all the right places.
It had us wondering where we'd been all our lives.

It had an uncanny resemblance
    to my girlfriend's family's coat of arms,
    which her father
    also bought through the mail.
Ours had a bridge, theirs had a swan.
Their name was Downing.
My girlfriend said Donald Downing came here in 1620.
She said their motto meant "The Swan Sits Firmly."
I knew we had a lot in common.

# At Sunset Palms

Poolside as the bright sun
settles behind these prickly
little mountains, we watch my son
snorkel for pennies. The pool's
all his right now, and he rolls
and glistens like an otter.

My father sits submerged
behind his eyes, gone
fishy since the operation,
his bony shoulders hanging down.
His fingers tap the chair arms
when my son shows us how deep
he can go, how long
he can stay under.
           Mother's nearly
round the stations of my childhood:
those five relentless tales
of the good boy and the bad,
how the bad boy once tried wading
in a swollen creek, how his mother
had to make a willow switch, how both
cried and cried.
           My father's
getting cold, but Mother keeps on
talking as if he's somewhere else,

still at war in Germany or at the office
late again. Maybe he is.
                              She says
he wakes her up all night,
shuffles into her room and bumps
the bed till she gets up,
that he can't do anything
for himself anymore, except
follow her around. And eat.

The fingers go on tapping
as my son tries a suicide
and comes up beaming. Mother
doesn't see him. "Last night,"
she announces, "he told me
he wasn't going to die."

## The Kiss of Death

is a family kiss, blood to blood,
Michael Corleone
gripping brother Fredo
by the chops
and planting a big one
to signify the ancient meaning:
"You're fucking dead/
I love you,"
the original mixed message,
passed branch to branch
up the family weeping willow,
since Cain and Absalom,

like the last kiss
I gave my father,
lightly on his forehead
as he lay gowned and diapered
in his last room, his skin
damp, his mind cornered
by something bad come home
to grill him every waking hour,

maybe by the dream I had,
where I finally threw a punch,
then kept it up till blood
leaked out his ears and I snapped
awake,

or maybe by a dream he had
about his father, that mostly
loving man he said would sometimes
punish with a razor strop
—once till Grandma screamed—
and kiss him afterwards.
My father taught himself
to flail with words
and silences. His kisses stabbed.

"I love you, Dad," I lied
to no one in particular before I left,
wiping off the blade,
meaning every word.

# Visit

*—Georgetown Medical Center, 1991*

The place looks dingy, like the rest of D.C.
By the nurses' station, an old black man
cinched in a wheelchair heaves his torso forward,
lurches and lurches, trying to work his way
to the heavy double doors marked EXIT, unaware
of a belt that anchors him to the handrail on the wall.
He frets in silence, unlike his hallmate at the far end,
a tiny crone who could pass for his twin, berating
someone only she can see. "*You* hush!" she squawks,
eyes fiery, then dead.
     I enter 803,
where my mother's propped in an ancient lounger, a sheet
to cover where the gown leaves off, the TV yammering
on Low. Two of my sister's children sit
before her offering memories, trying for one
that takes—something friendly and familiar,
easy to hold onto: the house on Bouchelle Avenue,
her matchless sponge cake, her new silk dress,
her great-granddaughter's morning antics.
But her liver's leaking poisons to her brain.
        "Billy

rilly pilly gilly pilly rilly,"
she complains, turning toward me and holding out
her needle-bruised arms. I'm a child again,
lost in the grocery store; I'm her father, who's heard
something shatter upstairs where she was playing

and come to see what's wrong. Everything's wrong:
the skull and bones already showing through,
her feet swollen into two crooked boots,
her pampered hair tufted and dull.
        "Come on."
she says, fluttering her outstretched hands, lunging
forward to rise. "Come on. Come on. Let's go!"
She presses non-stop till I raise the chair
and lift her to her feet. We stand there, teetering some
like awkward, mismatched pupils in a dancing class,
her, staring past my chest to the door.
Then we're on our way, edging out
and along the handrail, laboring at first
but, soon, steadier, pushing the pace, now
turning heads, drawing comments from the nurses.
"Can't keep Mildred down," they croon. "Atta girl."
She's the sweetheart of the ward, the debutante of dying's
slippery pit, till she stops, says she's tired,
and we sidestep back to where we started.
        "Come on,
come on!" she snaps as soon as I sit her down.
She pouts, calls us chicken shits, says
she can't believe this after all she's done
for us. So I help her up again, six more times,
her jaw set, her neck stiff as she wills
dead feet to rise and step, till all's
spent, and she lets me lift her into bed,
then drowses off.
     The granddaughters go; I linger
awhile, listen to her easy, sleeper's breaths.
Then, slipping out, I see the old man's

loose and nearly to the door, leather face
rapt as a winning marathoner's, till a nurse
strolls over, turns him around, and wheels him back.

The doors thump shut behind me as I stride
toward the still bright afternoon.

# In Memoriam: Duffy

*1979–1995*

Like most old dogs, you were content
to snooze the day, to perk up only
at the smell of food or shit, the receding
sound of someone at the door, the blearing
outline of squirrel or jay, or the prospect
of your last clear pleasures: ear scratch and belly rub
—and of course to do the dying by yourself,
sometimes looking deep in thought,
though no doubt thinking little past
the latest square of sunlight on the rug.
You left the fretting up to us, the fretters,
with our sermons and our burial vaults,
our rules for where to piss, for when
and what to eat, who scolded when you
brought the road-kill bunny home,
who slapped your nose when you chased
the next door brat into the street.
                              Finally,
the bone-shaped treat you danced the buck
and wing for every morning in the kitchen
lay for days beside your water dish and rubber frog,
and the car ride to the vet that always scared you
operatic barely caught your notice. You left us
as you came: one lick, then off to what comes next.

# The Band Director's Farewell

Some say he's not all there now, but here's
what's left of however much there might have been,
seated on the makeshift dais in the cafeteria,
smiling at the yellow wall behind us
while the superintendent grips the lectern
to intone the irreplaceability
of whom this gathering confirms will be replaced.

We hauled our children to him for the rudiments
of trumpet, snare, and sousaphone till neither
we nor they could stand another note.
He could, mostly smiled through the blats
and tweedles of each afternoon, though sometimes
grew a touch cantankerous, a little
too much maestro for the Marching Ducks,
and lately seemed to slip inside himself
and close the door. Some illness? Anyway,
the program's close to its finale; time
for him to get the hand and let us go
before we start to fidget like some bunch
from seventh hour strangling the Ode to Joy.

## Box Kite

In one of the photos
we've saved of her,
my daughter holds
the string in both hands
above her head to gain
an extra foot of sky. "Oh,
it's up," she's saying,
small frame torqued
with hope and English
as the frail contraption, unlikely
as a flying apple crate,
proclaims lightheartedness
above the power poles
and treetops.
          I feel the string
extend into the traffic up there,
into the flyways and airwaves,
transmitting the chill and chatter,
the enterprise and loose change,
the sweep of blue extravagance
to her fingers from the altitude
I reached when I had her grip:
ionospheric, I'd swear, cosmic,
the red box growing tiny
and remote as a moment
in the past can seem and big
as Kitty Hawk, as Icarus.

# Cadillac

*"Water commin in underneath the hood;*
*knew that was doin my motor good."*
—Chuck Berry

Prerequisite for limousine
or hearse, what gave
the doo-wop group their name,
what instituted fins
for generations, what Elvis
bought his furniture to match,
said fat pretender
to my friends and me,
who knew that Chuck,
when he caught Maybellene
in that Coupe DeVille,
did it in a V-8 Ford.

In '57 the bible,
*Mad,* christened
a broken shin
from one of those
nose cones jutting
from the bumper
the "Dagmar Fracture,"
after a famous 50s
double-D cup. "Park
that baby anywhere,
and it says something,"
said my father, who,

after moving up,
bought one every
other year: sun-gold
El Dorado that glistered
in our neighbors' eyes.

I watch the latest ad:
"You've paid your dues,"
croons a voice as Fortune
and her latest beau, bronzed
and willowy as tennis pros,
take Highway 1, Big Sur
to Carmel. I can almost
feel the cash-flow
in what hair I've got, smell
the surf and Simonize, till
I close my eyes. Swerving
off a back street
out of East St. Louis,
Plenty and his bawd
roar past them in a dented Ford,
laughter trailing
like a long, gaudy flag.

# Suckers

*"Go to Mr. Snopes at the store. . . . He will lend it to*
*you. He lent me five dollars over two years ago and all I*
*does, every Saturday night I goes to the store and pays*
*him a dime. He ain't even mentioned that five dollars."*
                                    —The Hamlet

We've got a bet and a punch named after us: "Look
over there," they say, "at the monkey." And we do.
"Double or nothing?" we're asked. "Sure," we say,
"what've I got to lose." Take my father,
who'd pay top dollar for a "special" deal,
go all out for "inside" information,
for the "limited" offer; who was sold the deluxe
-bound Harvard Classics, a family coat of arms,
two acres of Rancho Alkaline. He couldn't beat
the market—bought with gold, sold for copper:
Packard, Braniff. He wanted "something jazzy"
out of life, something that made him feel
"first class," which, he loved the chance to say,
"costs very little more to go." I bought it
early, sending my dimes and box tops
off to Battle Creek for the Captain Video
Flying Saucer Ring, the Lone Ranger six-gun
flashlight. I played the 120-bass accordion,
football at 140 pounds, the high-school fool
for love. In college, I majored in philosophy,
then switched to English, damn near
joined the Marines in '65, would have
if my father, who'd spent a year ducking

shrapnel in Luxembourg and Germany
had said anything but "WHAT?"

Now I live by the chalkboard and the pen,
hang around with that bunch who's mostly
last when it comes to salary and leverage,
first when the state decides to round up
the subversives. Paint "Something Jazzy"
on the trap and you'll catch us every time. "Why
can't you ever learn?" the unillusioned ask,
crouched along the bottom line. We shrug,
smile, and carry on, passing up
the even breaks, born every minute.

# Curtain Call

At last they stand together, flushed,
reborn, bathed in our applause: York,
Clarence, Ann, the little princes, and,
all self-effacing smiles, Richard himself,
gone straight as anyone, an actor like the rest,
who now hold hands with him, all as fresh
from mocking death as the magician's helper
who leapt before us from the hilt-encrusted box
or our father, who, the time his corpse act
got too real for us, raised his head and grinned.
For a moment it seems he might be here,
on stage with the others, with our mother,
with a whole growing cast of those we loved
or didn't, still in makeup and costume
to show the wounds, the sicknesses are void,
the years imaginary. We grin like fools,
smack our hands together till they sting.